MATH TRAILBLAZERS™

GRADE 1

SECOND EDITION

Student Guide
Book One

A Mathematical Journey Using Science and Language Arts

KENDALL/HUNT PUBLISHING COMPANY
4050 Westmark Drive   Dubuque, Iowa 52002

A TIMS® Curriculum
University of Illinois at Chicago

MATH TRAILBLAZERS™

Dedication

This book is dedicated to
the children and teachers
who let us see the magic
in their classrooms
and to our families who
wholeheartedly
supported us while we
searched for
ways to make it happen.

The TIMS Project

 UIC The University of Illinois
at Chicago

The original edition was based on work supported by the National Science Foundation under grant No. MDR 9050226 and the University of Illinois at Chicago. Any opinions, findings, and conclusions or recommendations expressed in this publication are those of the authors and do not necessarily reflect the views of the granting agencies.

Acknowledgments

Teaching Integrated Mathematics and Science (TIMS) Project Directors

Philip Wagreich, Principal Investigator
Joan L. Bieler
Marty Gartzman
Howard Goldberg (emeritus)
Catherine Randall Kelso

Director, Second Edition

Catherine Randall Kelso

Curriculum Developers, Second Edition

Lindy M. Chambers-Boucher
Elizabeth Colligan
Marty Gartzman
Carol Inzerillo

Catherine Randall Kelso
Georganne E. Marsh
Leona Peters
Philip Wagreich

Editorial and Production Staff, Second Edition

Kathleen R. Anderson
Ai-Ai C. Cojuangco
Andrada Costoiu
Erika Larson
Georganne E. Marsh
Cosmina Menghes
Anne Roby

TIMS Professional Developers

Barbara Crum
Craig Cleve
Elizabeth Colligan
Pamela Guyton

Carol Inzerillo
Linda Miceli
Leona Peters
Jane Schlichting

TIMS Director of Media Services

Henrique Cirne-Lima

TIMS Research Staff

Catherine Randall Kelso
Barry Booton
Dibyen Majumdar

TIMS Administrative Staff

Ora Benton
David Cirillo
Enrique Puente

Principal Investigators, First Edition

Philip Wagreich, Project Director
Howard Goldberg

Acknowledgments

Senior Curriculum Developers, First Edition

Janet Simpson Beissinger
Joan L. Bieler
Astrida Cirulis
Marty Gartzman
Howard Goldberg

Carol Inzerillo
Andy Isaacs
Catherine Randall Kelso
Leona Peters
Philip Wagreich

Curriculum Developers, First Edition

Janice C. Banasiak
Lynne Beauprez
Andy Carter
Lindy M. Chambers-Boucher
Kathryn Chval
Diane Czerwinski

Jenny Knight
Sandy Niemiera
Janice Ozima
Polly Tangora
Paul Trafton

Illustrator, First Edition

Kris Dresen

Research Consultant, First Edition

Andy Isaacs

Mathematics Education Consultant, First Edition

Paul Trafton

National Advisory Committee, First Edition

Carl Berger
Tom Berger
Hugh Burkhardt
Donald Chambers
Naomi Fisher
Glenda Lappan

Mary Lindquist
Eugene Maier
Lourdes Monteagudo
Elizabeth Phillips
Thomas Post

Table of Contents

Additional student pages may be found in the *Adventure Book*
or the *Unit Resource Guide*.

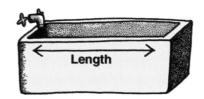

Length

Table of Contents

Additional student pages may be found in the *Adventure Book* or the *Unit Resource Guide*.

Letter to Parents

Dear Parents,

Math Trailblazers™ is based on the ideas that mathematics is best learned through solving many different kinds of problems and that all children deserve a challenging mathematics curriculum. The program provides a careful balance of concepts and skills. Traditional arithmetic skills and procedures are covered through their repeated use in problems and through distributed practice. *Math Trailblazers,* however, offers much more. Students using this program will become proficient problem solvers, will know when and how to apply the mathematics they have learned, and will be able to clearly communicate their mathematical knowledge. Computation, measurement, geometry, data collection and analysis, estimation, graphing, patterns and relationships, mental arithmetic, and simple algebraic ideas are all an integral part of the curriculum. They will see connections between the mathematics learned in school and the mathematics used in everyday life. And, they will enjoy and value the work they do in mathematics.

The *Student Guide* is only one component of *Math Trailblazers.* Additional material and lessons are contained in the *Adventure Book* and in the teacher's *Unit Resource Guides.* If you have questions about the program, we encourage you to speak with your child's teacher.

This curriculum was built around national recommendations for improving mathematics instruction in American schools and the research that supported those recommendations. The first edition was extensively tested with thousands of children in dozens of classrooms over five years of development. In preparing this second edition, we have benefited from the comments and suggestions of hundreds of teachers and children who have used the curriculum. *Math Trailblazers* reflects our view of a complete and well-balanced mathematics program that will prepare children for the 21st century—a world in which mathematical skills will be important in most occupations and mathematical reasoning will be essential for acting as an informed citizen in a democratic society. We hope that you enjoy this exciting approach to learning mathematics and that you watch your child's mathematical abilities grow throughout the year.

Philip Wagreich

Philip Wagreich
Professor, Department of Mathematics, Statistics, and Computer Science
Director, Institute for Mathematics and Science Education
The *Math Trailblazers* Team
Teaching Integrated Mathematics and Science (TIMS) Project
University of Illinois at Chicago

Unit 1

WELCOME TO FIRST GRADE

	Student Guide	Adventure Book	Unit Resource Guide*
Lesson 1			
Look Around You		◎	
Lesson 2			
We're Counting on You!	◎		
Lesson 3			
The Train Game			
Lesson 4			
More or Less	◎		

Unit Resource Guide pages are from the teacher materials.

Counting at the Toy Store

How Many Are There?

Count objects on the *Counting at the Toy Store* Activity Page.

Object	Number Counted
clock	
horse	
teddy bear	
supercycle	
doll	

In My Home

Homework

Dear Family Member:

Your child is learning to count objects. Help your child complete the table below.

Thank you for your cooperation.

Select and count objects such as clocks or shoes around your home. Write or draw each object in the table below. Record the number counted.

Object I Counted	Number

Measuring with Six Links

Compare your chain of six links with objects in the room. Decide if each object is *more than, less than,* or *about the same* as six links. Complete the table.

Object	Circle One
	More Less About the same
	More Less About the same
	More Less About the same
	More Less About the same
	More Less About the same
	More Less About the same

Six Links at Home

Homework

Dear Family Member:

We are studying the ideas of *more than, less than,* and *about the same*. Please help your child complete the table below.

Thank you for your cooperation.

Write or draw five household objects in the table below. After comparing the lengths of these objects with the picture of six links on the right, circle "more," "less," or "about the same."

Object	Circle One
	More **Less** **About the same**
	More **Less** **About the same**
	More **Less** **About the same**
	More **Less** **About the same**
	More **Less** **About the same**

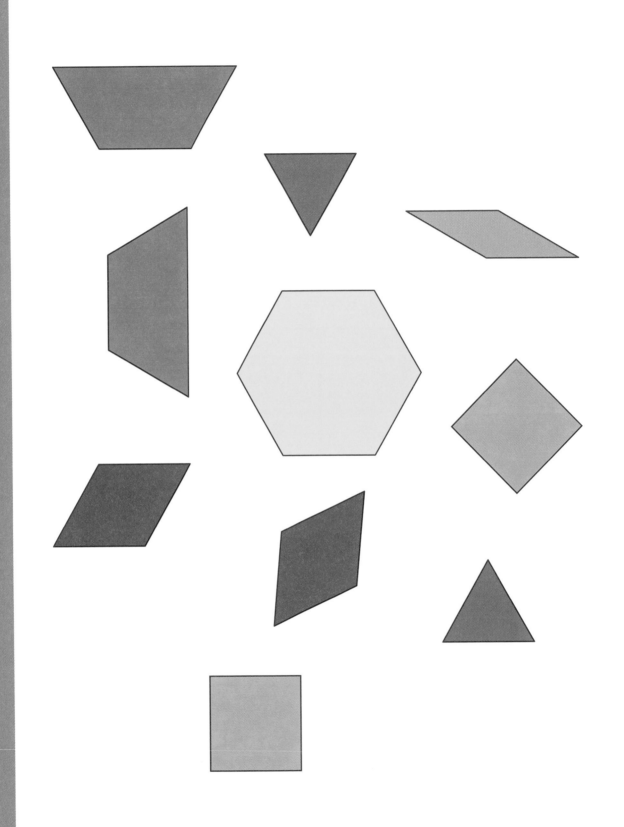

Unit 2
Exploring Shapes

	Student Guide	Adventure Book	Unit Resource Guide*
Lesson 1			
Shapes Around Us			
Lesson 2			
Describing Shapes	◎		
Lesson 3			
Seven Ways to Make a Hexagon	◎		
Lesson 4			
How Many Does It Take?	◎		
Lesson 5			
Mystery Figure			
Lesson 6			
Weather 1: Eye on the Sky	◎		◎

Unit Resource Guide pages are from the teacher materials.

Shapes in Nature

Nature is filled with shapes. Circle the shapes you see in the picture.

Nancy's Apartment and Yard

Homework

Dear Family Member:

Please help your child outline each shape using the colors indicated below. Then, help him or her complete the table.

Thank you for your cooperation.

Find all the shapes below.

Outline all △s with red, ▢s with blue, ◯s with green, and ▭s with yellow.

How many of each shape do you see?

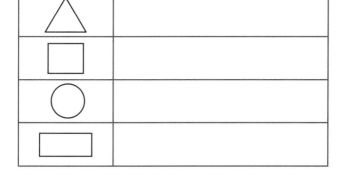

Alike and Different 1

One way these shapes are alike:

_____

One way these shapes are different:

_____

One way these shapes are alike:

_____

One way these shapes are different:

_____

Alike and Different 2

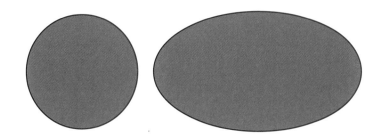

One way these shapes are alike:

_____

One way these shapes are different:

_____

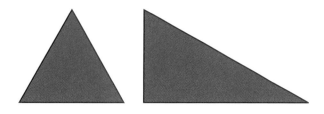

One way these shapes are alike:

_____

One way these shapes are different:

_____

First Grade Times

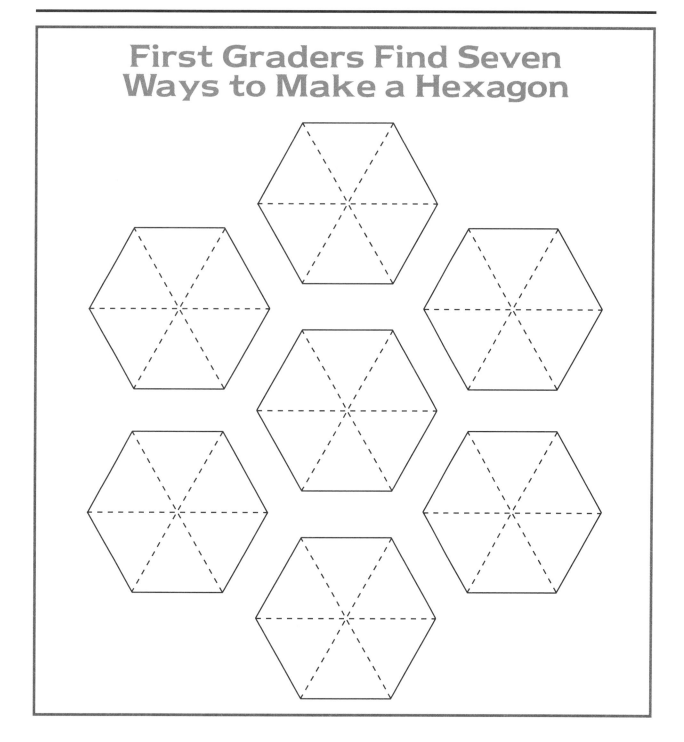

First Graders Find Seven Ways to Make a Hexagon

The Snake

Fill in the snake with pattern blocks.

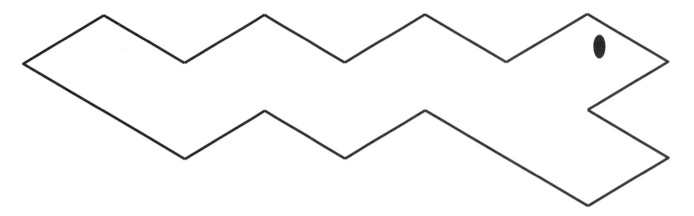

Write how many of each pattern block you used.

Shape	First Way	Second Way	Third Way
⬡			
⬢			
▲			
▪			
▱			
▱			
Total			

The Turtle

Fill in the turtle with pattern blocks.

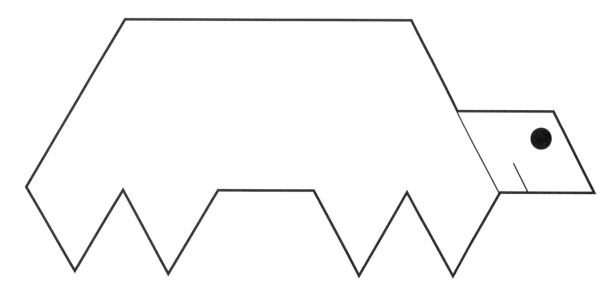

Write how many of each pattern block you used.

Shape	First Way	Second Way	Third Way
⬡			
⬢			
▲			
■			
▰			
▱			
Total			

My Own Design

Make a design with pattern blocks in the frame below.

I made a picture of _____

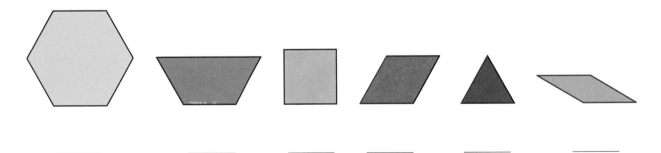

_____   _____   _____   _____   _____   _____

The Rocket

Fill in the rocket with pattern blocks. Then, write how many of each pattern block you used.

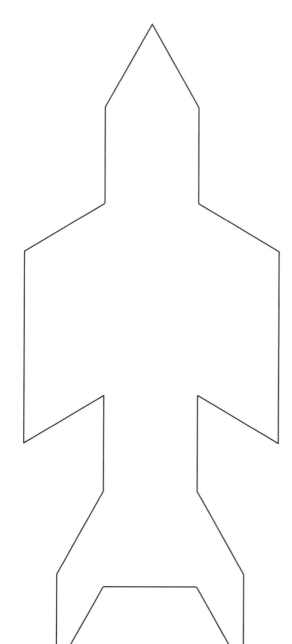

Shape	First Way	Second Way
⬡		
⬢		
▲		
◻		
▰		
▱		
Total		

Name _____ Date _____

Weather Calendar

Time of Day: 🕐

Month: _____   Year: _____

Sunday	Monday	Tuesday	Wednesday	Thursday	Friday	Saturday

Weather 1 Data Table

Collect

Record the data from your *Weather Calendar* in the table below.

T Type of _____	*N* Number of _____	
	Tallies	Total

Weather 1 Graph

Graph

Make a graph of your data.

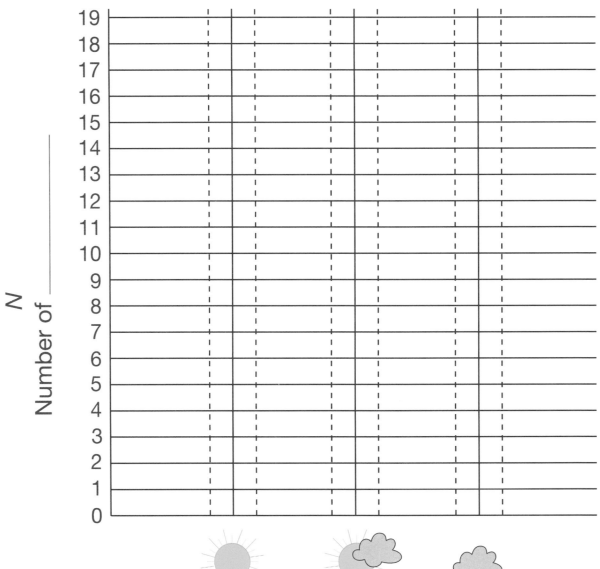

N
Number of _____

T

Type of _____

Thinking about the Weather

Use your data table and graph to answer the following questions.

1. Which type of sky did you see *most* often?

_____

2. Which type of sky did you see *least* often?

_____

3. How many sunny *and* partly sunny skies were there in all?

_____

4. A. Were there more cloudy skies or more sunny skies?

_____

B. How many more?

_____

Unit 3
PENNIES, POCKETS, AND PARTS

	Student Guide	Adventure Book	Unit Resource Guide*
Lesson 1			
Favorite Colors	@		
Lesson 2			
Ten Frames	@		
Lesson 3			
Think and Spin	@		
Lesson 4			
Pockets Graph			
Lesson 5			
Pocket Parts	@		@
Lesson 6			
What's in That Pocket?	@		
Lesson 7			
Purchasing with Pennies	@		

*Unit Resource Guide pages are from the teacher materials.

Kitchen Tools

Homework

Dear Family Member:

We have been thinking about numbers and tallies. Please help your child count and tally the objects below.

For example: ~~IIII~~ II   for seven

Ask questions that will stimulate your child's thinking:

* How many plates and forks are there altogether?

* How many more cups than forks are there?

Count and tally the objects in the table.

Objects	Tallies	Total

House Walk

Homework

Dear Family Member:

Please help your child count the objects listed in the table. As you go from room to room, have your child record a tally for each object he or she sees. After all of the rooms have been checked, have your child count the tallies and record the total.

Thank you for your cooperation.

Record a tally for each object in your home. Then, count the tallies and record the total.

Object	Tallies	Total
Lamp		
Chair		
Table		
Clock		
Window		

Ten Frames

What's My Number?

Write the number of counters in each question on the line.

1.

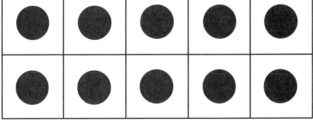

_____

2.

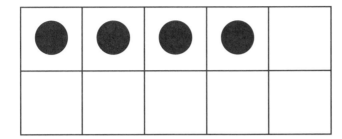

_____

3.

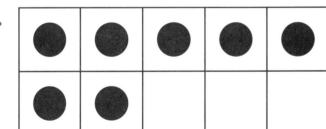

_____

4.

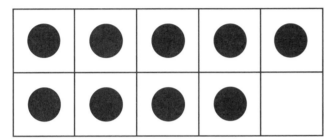

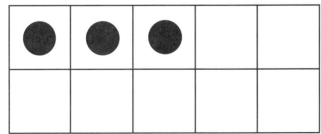

_____

Number Sentences

Write a number sentence for each question.

1.

⬛⬛⬛⬛⬛
⬛⬛⬛◻◻

☐ + ☐ = ☐

2.

⬛⬛⬛⬛⬛
◻◻◻◻◻

☐ + ☐ = ☐

3.

⬛⬛⬛⬛⬛
⬛⬛⬛⬛◻

☐ + ☐ = ☐

4.

⬛⬛⬛⬛⬛
⬛⬛⬛⬛⬛

⬛⬛⬛⬛⬛
◻◻◻◻◻

☐ + ☐ = ☐

What's My Sentence?

Write a number sentence for each question.

1.

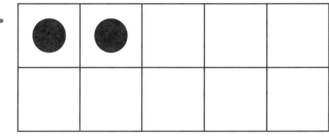

☐ + ☐ = ☐

2.

☐ + ☐ = ☐

3.

☐ + ☐ = ☐

4.

☐ + ☐ = ☐

Think and Spin

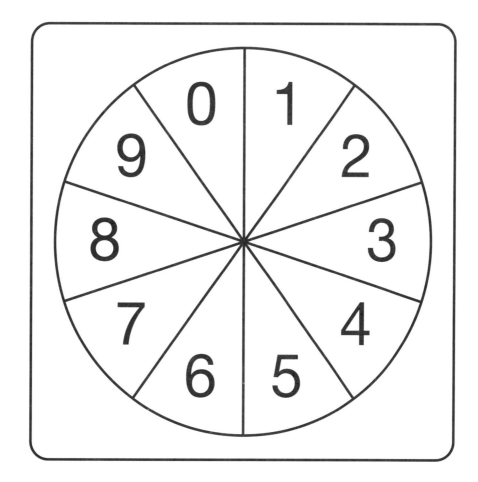

Ten Frame Recording Sheet

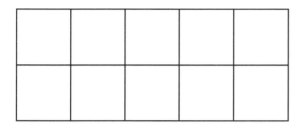

_____

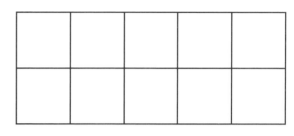

_____

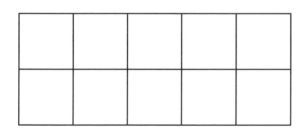

_____

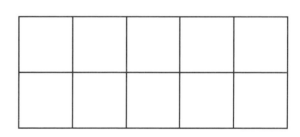

_____

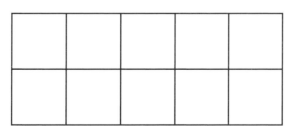

_____

Wearing Pockets

Homework

Dear Family Member:

Tomorrow your child will gather data and make a bar graph. We will count the number of pockets on each student's clothing. Please help your child select clothing that has pockets on the pants, skirt, or shirt.

Thank you for your cooperation.

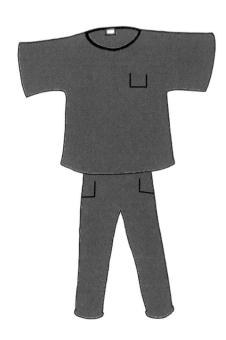

Shirt and Pants Pockets

Record the number of shirt pockets, pants pockets, and total pockets you are wearing today. Then, write a number sentence.

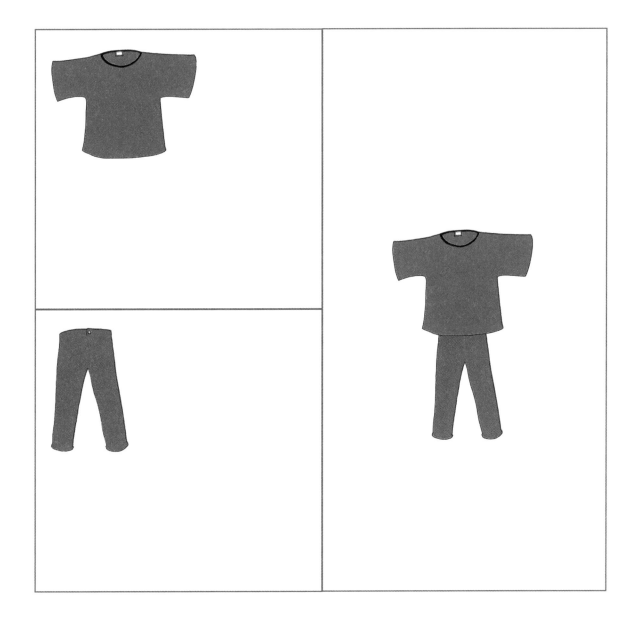

$$\boxed{} + \boxed{} = \boxed{}$$

Pocket Parts 1

Find the total number of pockets. Then, write a number sentence for each.

1.

1 + 4 = 5

2.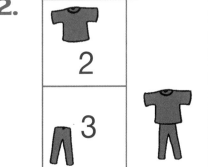

3.

4.

5.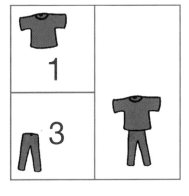

6.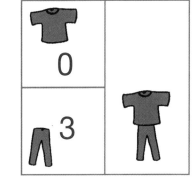

Pocket Parts 2

Find the total number of pockets for each. Then, write a number sentence for each.

1.

_____ 4 + 4 = _____

2.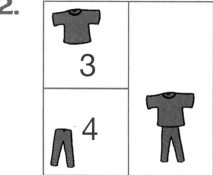

3.

_____

4.

_____

5.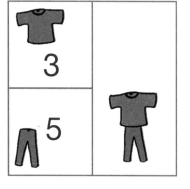

_____

6.

_____

Pocket Parts

How Many Pockets?

Find the total number of pockets for each. Then, write a number sentence to show the three parts and the whole.

1.

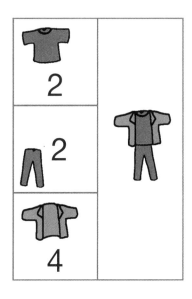

$2 + 2 + 4 = 8$

2.

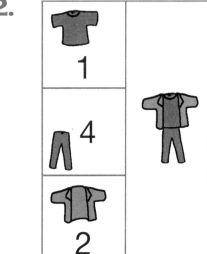

_____

3.

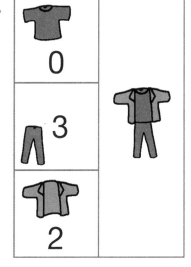

_____

4.

_____

Hidden Pockets

Find the number of pants pockets for each student. Then, write a number sentence for each.

1.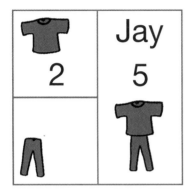

Jay
2
5

$2 + 3 = 5$

2.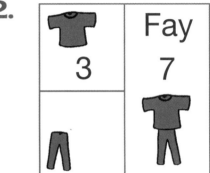

Fay
3
7

_____

3.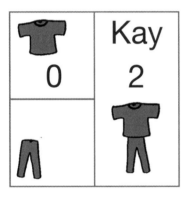

Kay
0
2

_____

4.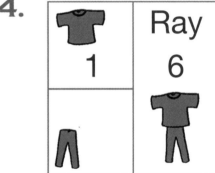

Ray
1
6

_____

5.

May
2
4

_____

6.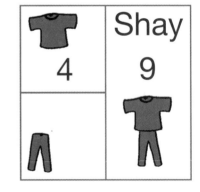

Shay
4
9

_____

Pockets

Find the missing number or the total number of pockets for each. Then, write a number sentence for each.

1.

_____

2.

_____

3.
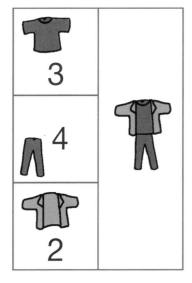

_____

4.
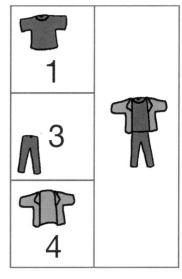

_____

Two Pockets Work Mat

Place your pennies on the pockets. Find and record the different ways you can arrange them.

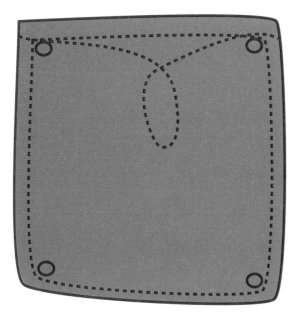

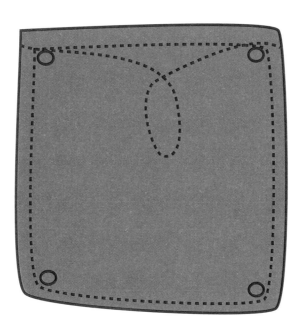

Two Pockets Data Table

How many ways can you arrange ten pennies in two pockets? Record as many ways as you can. Then, write a number sentence for each one.

		Total Pennies	Number Sentence

Three Pockets Work Mat

Place your pennies on the pockets. Find and record the different ways you can arrange them.

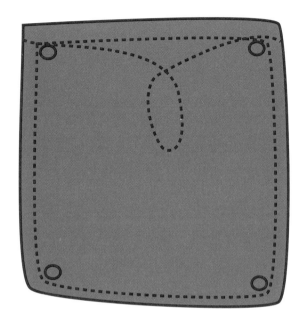

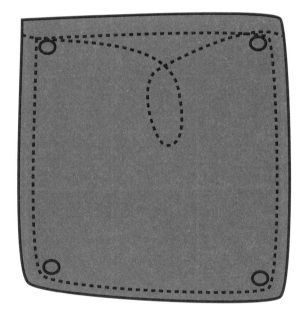

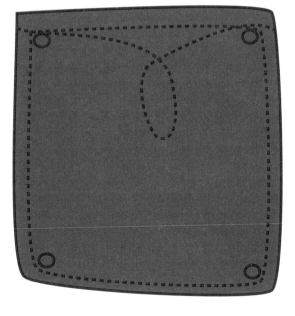

What's in That Pocket?

Three Pockets Data Table

How many ways can you arrange ten pennies in three pockets? Record as many ways as you can. Then, write a number sentence for each one.

			Total Pennies	Number Sentence
1	2	7	10	1 + 2 + 7 = 10

Name _____   Date _____

Eight Pennies Data Table

Homework

Dear Family Member:

Your child will need eight pennies for this assignment. He or she should divide the pennies in different combinations between two pockets. The total should equal eight for each problem. Please help your child complete the data table.

Thank you for your cooperation.

How many ways can you arrange eight pennies in two pockets? Record as many ways as you can. Then, write a number sentence for each one.

		Total Pennies	Number Sentence
0	8	8	0 + 8 = 8

Nine Pennies Data Table

How many ways can you arrange nine pennies in two pockets? Record as many ways as you can. Then, write a number sentence for each one.

		Total Pennies	Number Sentence

What Would I Buy?

Homework

Look at the items below.

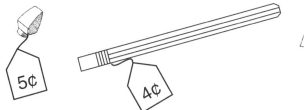  

1. Circle the items you would buy if you had ten pennies. (If you want two of the same item, make two circles around it.)

2. How much would you pay for all the items you circled? Show how you found your answer.

_____

3. Would you have any pennies left over? How many?

_____

4. Make up a problem for other students to solve.

_____

Unit 4

Adding to Solve Problems

	Student Guide	Adventure Book	Unit Resource Guide*
Lesson 1			
Exploring Even and Odd Numbers	◎		
Lesson 2			
The Pet Shop	◎		
Lesson 3			
Parts and Wholes	◎		◎
Lesson 4			
Counting On to Add	◎		

Unit Resource Guide pages are from the teacher materials.

Even or Odd?

1. Write a number for each picture.

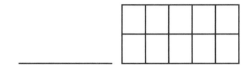

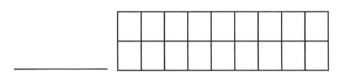

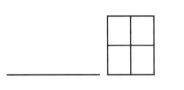

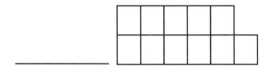

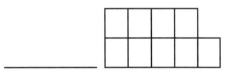

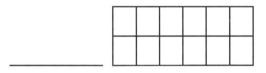

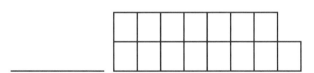

2. Circle the even numbers.
3. Look at the pictures above. Which numbers are odd?

_____

Name _____   Date _____

Is My Home Even or Odd?

Homework

Dear Family Member:

Your child is learning how to tell if a number of objects is even or odd. Help your child count the number of objects listed below. Record them in the table. Encourage him or her to show the number of each object with pennies or other counters. Your child should pair up the counters. If there is one leftover, the number is odd.

Example:

The number seven is odd because there is one leftover.

A number such as six is even because there are no leftovers.

Object	Number of Objects in My Home	Even or Odd
Chairs		Even or Odd
Rugs		Even or Odd
Lamps		Even or Odd
Tables		Even or Odd
Shoes		Even or Odd
Spoons		Even or Odd

Animals in the Pet Shop

Name _____   Date _____

Pets at Home

Use a calculator to solve the following problems.

1. Sylvia's block has three kittens and five puppies. How many pets are on Sylvia's block? Press the keystrokes below to find out.

| 3 | + | 5 | = |

2. For each problem, fill in the missing keystroke boxes. Then, find the answer.

A. Marcus's block has 5 dogs and 11 cats. How many dogs and cats do they have?

| 5 | + | | = |

B. Tom's family has 2 pets. There are 16 other pets in Tom's building. How many pets are in the building?

| | + | | = |

C. Marsha counted 12 dogs and 13 cats on her block. How many pets are there in all?

| | | | |

D. Samantha has two turtles, five frogs, and six lizards as pets. How many pets does Samantha have?

| | | | | | |

Animal Addition Stories

Homework

Dear Family Member:

Your child is writing and developing addition stories in the classroom. Help him or her write addition stories about animals. Include number sentences. Encourage your child to illustrate the stories.

Example:

Janice has two dogs and three cats in her home. She has five pets in all. (2 + 3 = 5)

Write three addition stories about animals. Draw a picture about your stories.

Addition Story 1:

_____

_____

_____

_____

Picture:

Addition Story 2:

_____

_____

_____

_____

Picture:

Addition Story 3:

_____

_____

_____

_____

Picture:

Parts and Wholes

I am showing different ways to make _____ .

✂ -

Part **Part**

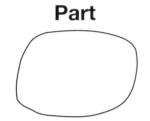 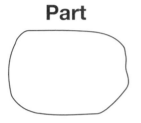

_____ + _____ = _____

✂ -

Part **Part**

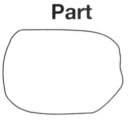 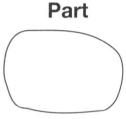

_____ = _____ + _____

✂ -

Part **Part** **Part**

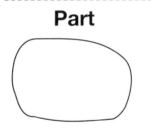 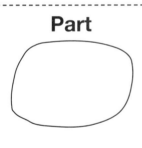 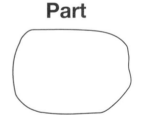

_____ + _____ + _____ = _____

✂ -

Part **Part** **Part**

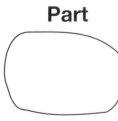 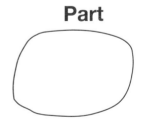 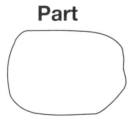

_____ = _____ + _____ + _____

It's in the Mail

Use the calendar to help you find the date the mail arrived.

Sunday	Monday	Tuesday	Wednesday	Thursday	Friday	Saturday
						1
2	3	4	5	6	7	8
9	10	11	12	13	14	15
16	17	18	19	20	21	22
23	24	25	26	27	28	29
30	31					

Date Sent	Arrived	Number Sentence	Date Received
10 mailed	3 days later	_____	☐
13 mailed	2 days later	_____	☐
24 mailed	4 days later	_____	☐
30 mailed	1 day later	_____	☐
5 mailed	5 days later	_____	☐
17 mailed	3 days later	_____	☐
20 mailed	5 days later	_____	☐
14 mailed	4 days later	_____	☐

Happy Helpers Club

Homework

Dear Family Member:

In class, your child uses the counting-on strategy to solve problems. To do 11 + 3, for example, start by saying "11" and then count on, "12, 13, 14." Encourage your child to use counting on to solve the problems below.

How much money will each student have after receiving 3 more cents?

13¢ + 3¢ = _____   18¢ + 3¢ = _____   20¢ + 3¢ = _____

24¢ + 3¢ = _____   29¢ + 3¢ = _____   32¢ + 3¢ = _____

Coin Jar

Homework

Dear Family Member:

Make a coin jar. Stock a small jar with a few nickels and about 20–30 pennies. Ask your child to remove a few coins from the coin jar. Help your child name the coins and find their value. Then, record the amount on the first purse. Repeat for each of the other purses.

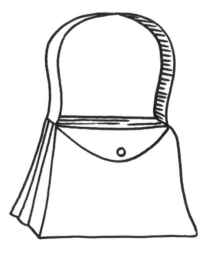

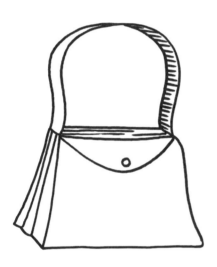
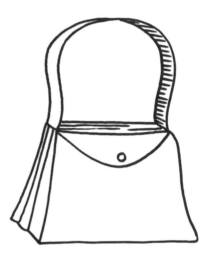
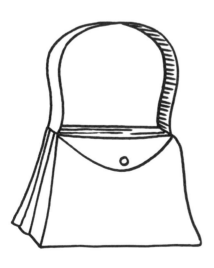

Unit 5
GROUPING AND COUNTING

	Student Guide	Adventure Book	Unit Resource Guide*
Lesson 1			
Skip Counting			
Lesson 2			
Counting by Fives and Tens	◎		
Lesson 3			
Sharing Cookies	◎		◎
Lesson 4			
I've Got a Little List		◎	
Lesson 5			
Colors	◎		◎

Unit Resource Guide pages are from the teacher materials.

Counting by Twos

Homework

A. Count the eyes by twos.

2, _____, _____   There are _____ eyes.

B. Count the bicycle wheels by twos.

2, _____, _____, _____, _____   There are _____ wheels.

C. Count the mittens by twos.

2, _____, _____, _____, _____, _____, _____

There are _____ mittens.

Things in Twos

Homework

Dear Family Member:

Your child is learning how to skip count by twos. Discuss things that come in groups of two such as wheels on a bicycle and ears. Have your child choose an object that comes in twos, draw several of them, and then count, in twos, the number he or she drew. Help him or her complete the bottom of the page.

Find things that come in twos. Then, draw and count them.

I counted twos like this:

2, _____, _____, _____, _____, _____, _____, _____, _____, _____, _____

What did you draw? _____

How many did you draw? _____

Ten Frames

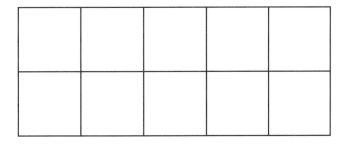

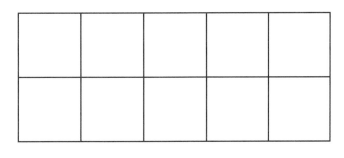

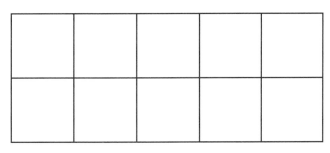

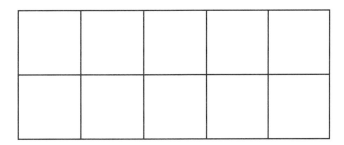

Fair Shares

Share cookies as shown in the table below.

The total number of cookies = _____

People	Fair Shares	Leftovers	Words
⚇ ⚇			Two groups of _____ and _____ left over
⚇ ⚇ ⚇			Three groups of _____ and _____ left over
⚇ ⚇ ⚇ ⚇			Four groups of _____ and _____ left over
⚇ ⚇ ⚇ ⚇ ⚇			Five groups of _____ and _____ left over
⚇ ⚇ ⚇ ⚇ ⚇ ⚇			Six groups of _____ and _____ left over

Packing Grandma's Cookies

Help Grandma pack her cookies. Group your counters in groups of ten. Draw one box for every group of ten. Then, draw the leftovers.

Work Slip 1	Number of Cookies	Boxes	Leftover Cookies

Work Slip 2	Number of Cookies	Boxes	Leftover Cookies

Cookie Factory

Homework

Dear Family Member:

Help your child group cookies in boxes of ten. Encourage him or her to draw the boxes and the leftover cookies. Your child may need counters such as beans to solve these problems.

Count, group, and box the cookies. Record your answers below.

		Number of Cookies	Boxes	Leftover Cookies
A.	Work Slip	22		
B.	Work Slip	26		
C.	Work Slip	35		
D.	Work Slip	39		
E.	Work Slip	50		

Colors Picture

Draw a picture of the experiment.

Colors Data Table

Collect

Total number of pieces in my sample _____

Colors

C Color	P Number of Pieces

Name _____   Date _____

Colors Graph

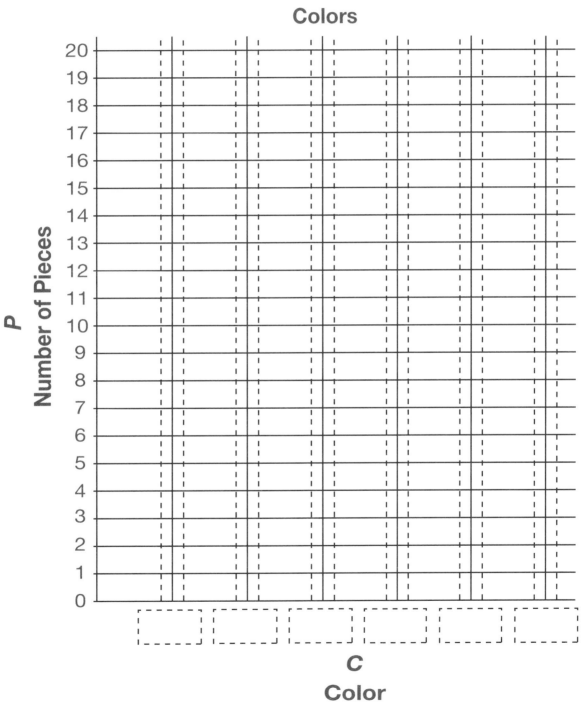

Colors

Number of Pieces

P

C
Color

Reading a Colors Graph

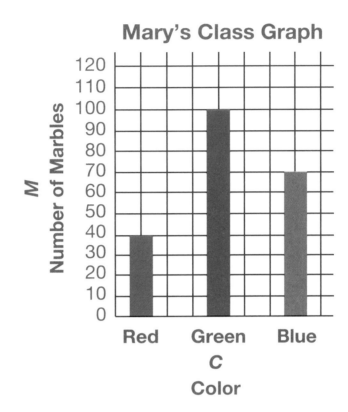

Mary's Class Graph

1. How many reds did Mary's class pull out altogether?

   _____

2. What color was most common? _____

3. If the principal took a handful of marbles, which color do you think she would find the most common?

   _____

4. If you combine the blues and the reds Mary's class pulled out, would they be more than the greens?

   _____

Unit 6

MEASUREMENT: LENGTH

	Student Guide	Adventure Book	Unit Resource Guide*
Lesson 1			
Linking Up	@		
Lesson 2			
Rolling Along with Links	@		
Lesson 3			
Betty Builds a Better Racer		@	
Lesson 4			
Using Unusual Units	@		
Lesson 5			
Delightful Dachshunds	@		
Lesson 6			
Give 'em an Inch	@		

Unit Resource Guide pages are from the teacher materials.

Measuring Our World

Here are some things in Maria's classroom. How do they compare with the same things in your classroom? Measure to find out.

Maria's desk is 18 links tall.

1. My desk is _____ links tall.

Maria's desk is 24 links long.

2. My desk is _____ links long.

Maria measured the distance around her math book. The distance around an object is called the **perimeter.**

The perimeter of Maria's math book is 39 links.

3. The perimeter of my *Student Guide*

is _____ links.

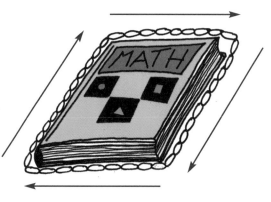

Measuring Ourselves

Julio's arm is 12 links long.

1. My arm is _____ links long.

Julio's foot is 5 links long.

2. My foot is _____ links long.

3. Use links to measure another part of your body. Draw a picture to show what you measure.

My _____ is _____ links long.

Rolling Along with Links

Draw a picture of the experiment setup. Include the parts of the experiment that must remain the same.

Collect

Record the distance each type of car rolled in the data table below.

Rolling Along with Links

T Type of Car	D Distance Rolled (in links)

Graph

Make a bar graph of your data. Remember to fill in the proper units.

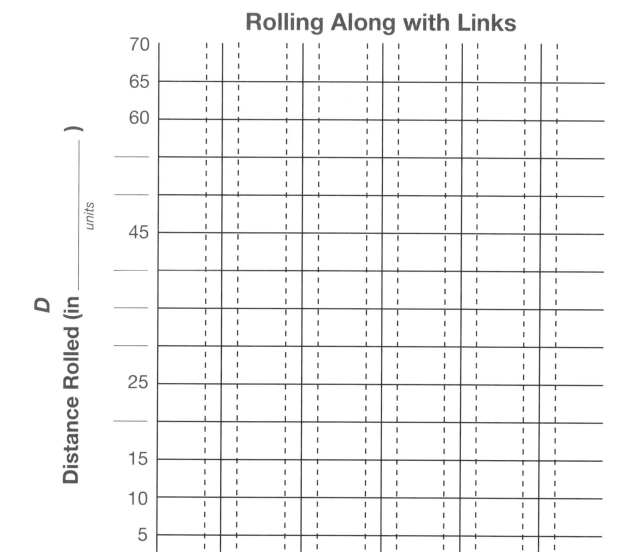

Rolling Along with Links

D
Distance Rolled (in _____)
units

T
Type of Car

Discuss

Use your data table and graph to answer the questions below.

1. Which car was the best roller? _____

2. How far did the best roller go? _____

3. Which car was the worst roller? _____

4. How far did the worst roller go? _____

5. How much farther did the best roller go than the worst roller? Discuss how you found your answer.

_____

6. Susan's car rolled 20 links. David's car rolled 12 links farther than Susan's. How far did David's car roll?

_____

7. Write a number sentence for your answer to Question 6.

_____

8. Tom's car rolled 17 links. Rico's car rolled 20 links. How much farther did Rico's car roll?

_____

9. Write a number sentence for your answer to Question 8.

_____

Two Car Roll-off

Homework

Dear Family Member:

Your child completed a lab where he or she rolled a car down a ramp and used links to measure the length the cars traveled. Help your child count the links in the picture below and complete the questions.

Two cars rolled from two ramps. In the drawing below, you are seeing the tops of the cars from above.

1. How far did car A roll? _____

2. How far did car B roll? _____

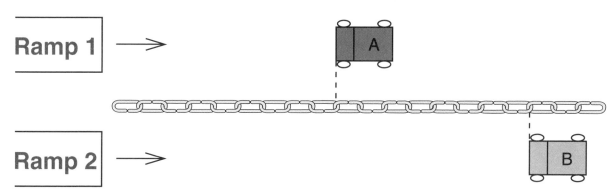

3. How much farther did car B roll than car A?

_____

4. Why might car B have rolled farther?

_____

_____

Brian's Class

Brian's class found the data shown in the graph below.

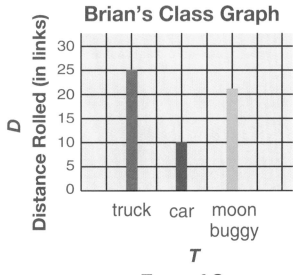

Brian's Class Graph

1. Which was the best roller?

_____

2. Which was the worst roller?

_____

3. How much farther did the truck travel than the car?

_____

4. About how far did the moon buggy roll?

_____

5. How much farther would the truck have to roll to reach a distance of 30 links?

_____

Watch Your Step

Use your footprint to measure distances in your classroom.
Record your measurements in this table.

From	To	Number of

Unusual Units

Estimate how many of each unit you need to measure the bathtub.

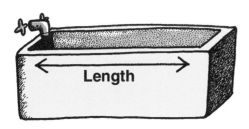

Length

Unit	Length of Tub
soap 🔲	_____
toothbrush	10
wash cloth	_____
towel	_____

It takes 3 soda pop bottles to measure the width of the refrigerator. Match the rest of the numbers with their units of measure.

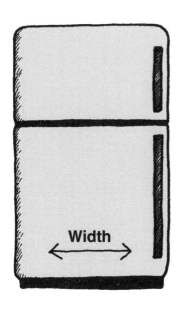

Width

Width of Refrigerator	Unit
12	• grape
9	2-liter soda pop
3	apple
35	margarine

Measuring at Home

Homework

Dear Family Member:

The boy in the picture is measuring a bed. He is using the edge of a paper towel as a unit. Help your child measure four things in your home using one object as the unit of measure. Some objects you might use as tools for measuring are a cooking utensil, a cereal box, a pencil, or a book.

Record your data in the table below.

Four Things Measured at Home

Things I Measured	Length Measured Using _____

Stepping Out with My Family

Homework

Dear Family Member:

Your child used footsteps to measure distances in the classroom. Encourage your child to measure straight distances in your home by counting his or her steps as your child walks "heel-to-toe." For example, your child might walk from the refrigerator to the kitchen table. Ask your child to write or draw pictures in the "From" and "To" columns to indicate the starting and stopping points. After your child measures and records the distances, ask him or her to predict the measurement if your footsteps were used. Check your child's prediction by measuring each distance using your footsteps. Ask your child to record your measurements.

Choose distances in your home, measure them, and record the data in the table below.

Distances in My Home

From	To	Number of My 👣	Number of Your 👣

Delightful Dachshunds

1. Which dog is longer? Make a prediction. Then, make link and cube chains to compare the lengths. Write the name of the dog in the box.

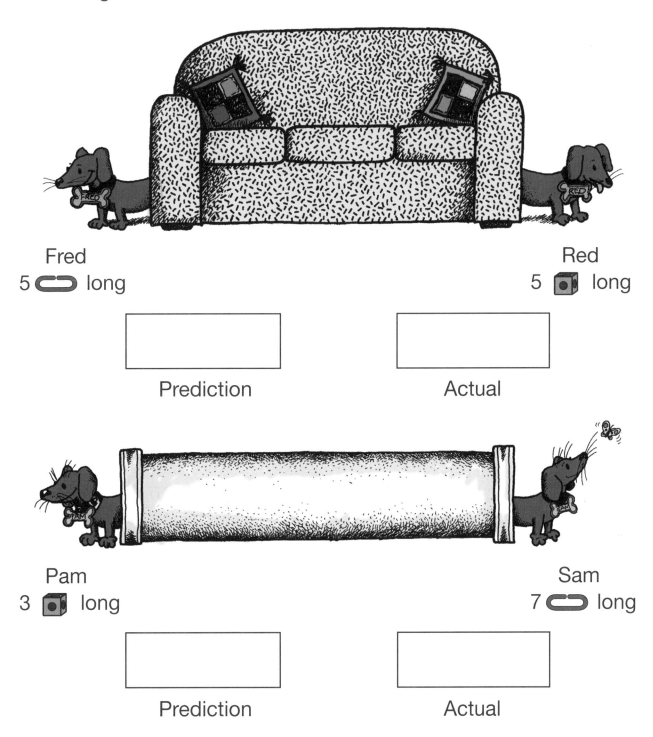

Fred
5 long

Red
5 long

Prediction	Actual

Pam
3 long

Sam
7 long

Prediction	Actual

Name _____ Date _____

Buddy
5 ⬭ long

Buster
6 🎲 long

┌──────────┐   ┌──────────┐
│   │   │   │
└──────────┘   └──────────┘
Prediction   Actual

2. Which length is longer? Make a prediction. Then, compare the lengths of the link and cube chains. Circle the longer one.

Prediction		Actual	
18 ⬭ long	25 🎲 long	18 ⬭ long	25 🎲 long
9 ⬭ long	8 🎲 long	9 ⬭ long	8 🎲 long
3 ⬭ long	7 🎲 long	3 ⬭ long	7 🎲 long
8 ⬭ long	12 🎲 long	8 ⬭ long	12 🎲 long

Comparing Links and Cubes

Predict the longer length. Make chains of links and trains of cubes. Then, circle the longer one.

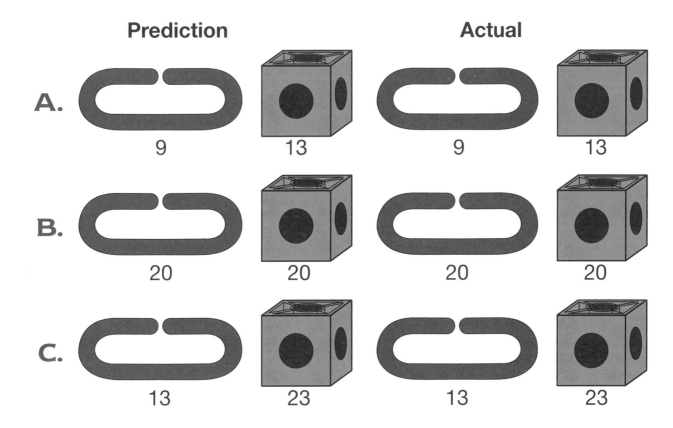

	Prediction		Actual	
A.	9	13	9	13
B.	20	20	20	20
C.	13	23	13	23

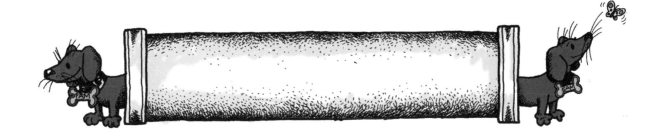

Could Be or Crazy?

Read each of the measurements below. Decide whether each one seems possible or crazy. Circle your answer. Use an inch ruler to help you decide.

1. A big toe is 5 inches long.

       could be   crazy

2. My teacher's foot is 10 inches long.

       could be   crazy

3. The length of a pencil is 20 inches.

       could be   crazy

4. The height of Bessie's doll is 25 inches.

       could be   crazy

5. Name something that could be 50 inches long.

_____

6. Name an object for which 50 inches is a crazy measurement.

_____

Unit 7
Patterns and Designs

	Student Guide	Adventure Book	Unit Resource Guide*
Lesson 1			
Line Up!	@		
Lesson 2			
Pick Apart a Pattern	@		
Lesson 3			
Name Patterns	@		
Lesson 4			
Pattern Block Symmetry	@		
Lesson 5			
Balancing Act	@		

Unit Resource Guide pages are from the teacher materials.

Name _____ Date _____

Translating and Recording Patterns

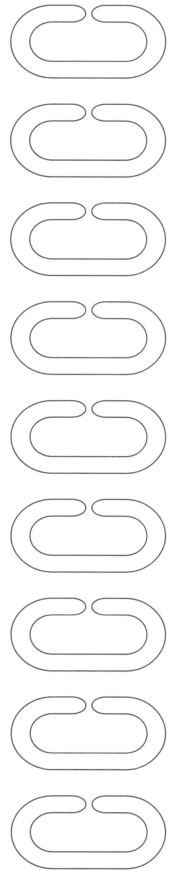
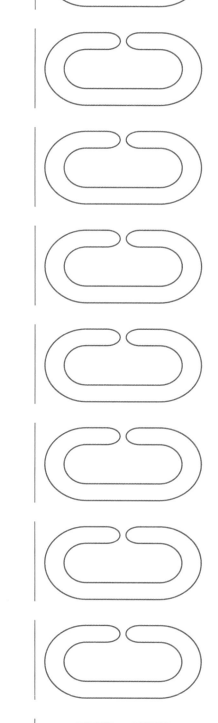

Copyright © Kendall/Hunt Publishing Company

Colors and Shapes

What patterns do you see?

Colors:

1.

2.

3.

Shapes:

4.

5.

6.

7.

8.

Dinosaurs, Diamonds, and Dog Biscuits

What patterns do you see?

1.

2.

3.

4.

5.

6.

7.

8.

Super Sleuth

Homework

Dear Family Member:

In this assignment, your child should find the part of the pattern that repeats itself and represent the pattern using the letters A, B, C, etc. For example, a boy-girl-boy-girl-boy-girl pattern is translated as ABABAB with letters.

Record the pattern shown on the lines below.

1.

_____

2.

_____

3.

_____

4.

_____

Twins

Write A, B, or C on the line under each object to show the pattern. Draw a ring around the repeating pattern unit.

1.

_____

2.

_____

3.

_____

4.

_____

Name Grid

Create a name grid pattern using your first name. Write one letter of your name in each box. Color the last letter of your name each time it occurs. Be careful not to skip any boxes.

Ten-by-Ten Name Grid

Homework

Dear Family Member:

Your child is learning about patterns in class. Help him or her create a name-grid pattern. Your child should fill in the grid by writing his or her first name many times. One letter of the name should be written in each box. Have your child color the last letter of his or her first name each time it occurs. Be careful not to skip any boxes.

Write your first name repeatedly in the boxes below.

Names and Grids

The last letter of the name will be in a shaded box.

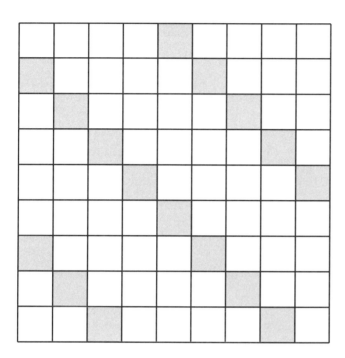

1. Circle the name that fits the pattern on this grid.

Maggie

Lynne

Van

Miko

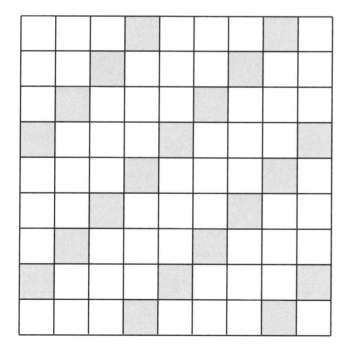

2. Write a name that fits the pattern on this grid.

_____

Trapezoid Man

1. Cover this side.   **2.** Make this side balance.

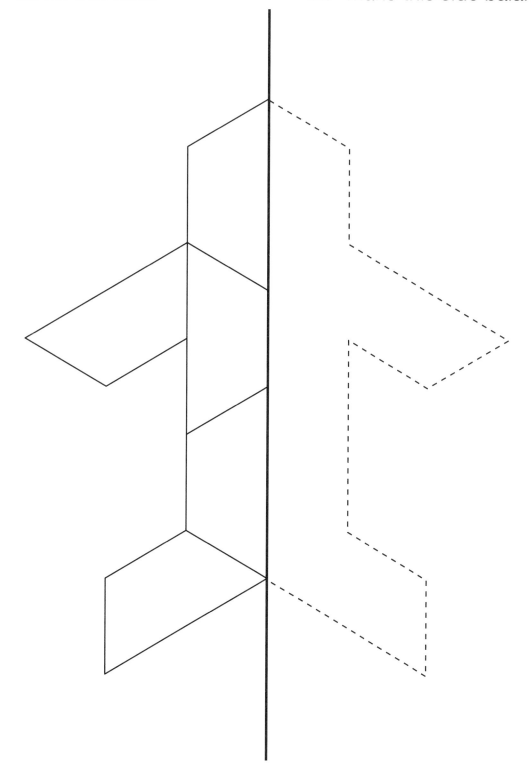

Butterfly

1. Cover this side.

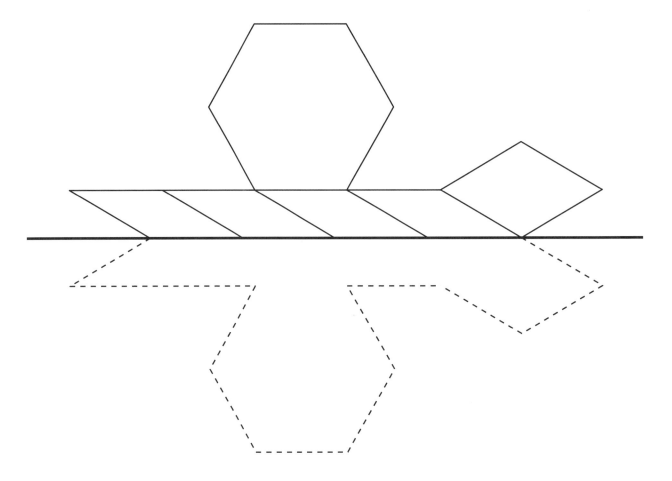

2. Make this side balance.

Pattern Block Symmetry

Van's Coin Jar

Homework

Dear Family Member:

Use a small jar of coins that contains nickels, dimes, and pennies.

Follow these steps:

1. Pull a few coins from the jar.

2. Find the value of the coins.

3. Record the amount on the data table in the My Coins column.

4. Repeat two more times.

Data Table

Pull	Van's Coins	My Coins
1	27¢	
2	34¢	
3	19¢	

Who pulled more money for each pull, Van or you? Circle the amount that shows more money.

Tree

1. Cover this side.   **2.** Make this side balance.

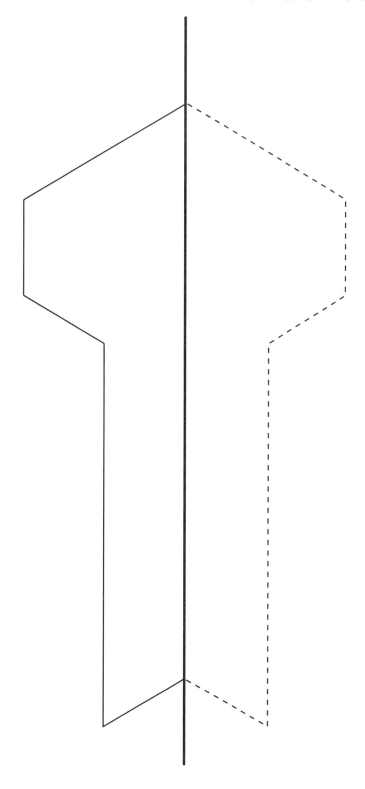

Balancing Act

Use pattern blocks to balance designs below.

Unit 8

SUBTRACTING TO SOLVE PROBLEMS

	Student Guide	Adventure Book	Unit Resource Guide*
Lesson 1			
At the Circus			
Lesson 2			
Our Own Stories	@		
Lesson 3			
Clowning Around	@		@
Lesson 4			
How Many in the Bag?	@		
Lesson 5			
Making Flip Books	@		@

*Unit Resource Guide pages are from the teacher materials.

Whole-Part-Part Mat

Whole

Part

Part

Recording Subtraction Sentences

_____ – _____ = _____
whole   part   part

_____ – _____ = _____
whole   part   part

_____ – _____ = _____
whole   part   part

_____ – _____ = _____
whole   part   part

_____ – _____ = _____
whole   part   part

_____ – _____ = _____
whole   part   part

_____ – _____ = _____
whole   part   part

_____ – _____ = _____
whole   part   part

Subtraction Story

Homework

Dear Family Member:

At school, we are working on subtraction problems by drawing pictures of take-away stories. Ask your child to tell a take-away story. Write down your child's story as he or she tells it to you. Your child should then illustrate the story and write a number sentence for it.

Thank you for your cooperation.

_____ − _____ = _____
     whole   *part*   *part*

Name _____ Date _____

Taking Home Subtraction Cartoons

Homework

Dear Family Member:

Your child illustrated a subtraction story in class. Encourage your child to illustrate another subtraction story based on a subtraction number sentence. Help your child choose an appropriate number sentence such as 9 − 4 = 5 or 12 − 3 = 9. Please ask your child to read the subtraction sentence and tell the story that he or she illustrates. You can help your child by asking him or her to identify the whole, the part that is taken away, and the part that is left.

Please send the subtraction cartoon story to school tomorrow so that your child can share it with the class.

Thank you for your cooperation.

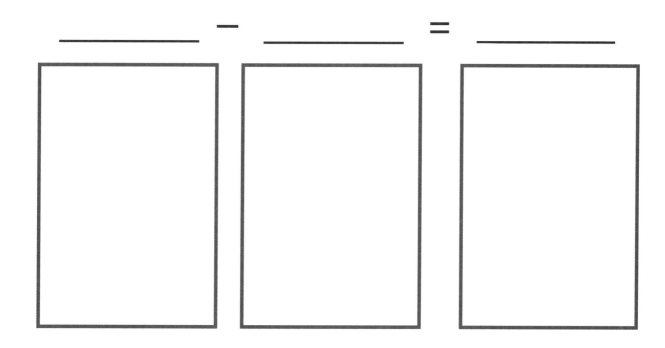

_____ − _____ = _____

How Many in the Bag?

_____ – _____ = _____
in the bag   taken out   left in the bag

_____ – _____ = _____
in the bag   taken out   left in the bag

_____ – _____ = _____
in the bag   taken out   left in the bag

_____ – _____ = _____
in the bag   taken out   left in the bag

_____ – _____ = _____
in the bag   taken out   left in the bag

_____ – _____ = _____
in the bag   taken out   left in the bag

_____ – _____ = _____
in the bag   taken out   left in the bag

_____ – _____ = _____
in the bag   taken out   left in the bag

Counting Up at Home

Homework

Dear Family Member:

In class, your child has been playing *How Many in the Bag?* with a partner. We would like you to play this game with your child. To play, you will need a bag and 20 beans (or other objects).

1. Put between 10 and 20 beans in a bag. Write the number of objects on the bag.

2. Pull out at least half of the beans, and place them on the table. Ask your child to count them.

3. Without looking in the bag, your child should figure out how many beans are left in the bag.

4. He or she should record the number sentence for this problem on the lines provided below and on the following page.

5. Repeat this activity until the lines are filled.

Ask your child how he or she found the answer. Children use many strategies for solving problems. One strategy often used by young children is called counting up. For example, if there are 14 beans in the bag and 11 are taken out, the child might count from 11 to 14 to find how many are left in the bag: "12, 13, 14." Since three more were counted, three is the answer.

Thank you for your cooperation.

_____ − _____ = _____
   in the bag   *taken out*   *left in the bag*

_____ − _____ = _____
   in the bag   *taken out*   *left in the bag*

_____ – _____ = _____
  in the bag   *taken out*   *left in the bag*

_____ – _____ = _____
  in the bag   *taken out*   *left in the bag*

_____ – _____ = _____
  in the bag   *taken out*   *left in the bag*

_____ – _____ = _____
  in the bag   *taken out*   *left in the bag*

_____ – _____ = _____
  in the bag   *taken out*   *left in the bag*

_____ – _____ = _____
  in the bag   *taken out*   *left in the bag*

Unit 9
GROUPING BY TENS

	Student Guide	Adventure Book	Unit Resource Guide*
Lesson 1			
Spill the Beans	@		
Lesson 2			
More or Less than 100?	@		
Lesson 3			
Spin for Beans	@		@
Lesson 4			
The *50 Chart*	@		@
Lesson 5			
The *100 Chart*	@		@
Lesson 6			
Measuring with Connecting Links	@		
Lesson 7			
Numbers in the News	@		@
Lesson 8			
Full of Beans	@		

Unit Resource Guide pages are from the teacher materials.

Group and Count

Homework

Dear Family Member:

In class, we are counting by grouping objects in tens and leftover ones. You can help provide additional practice for your child by gathering a collection of objects and setting it out for your child to group and count. Change the total number of objects at least two times. Some ideas for objects to use are cereal pieces, nuts, pasta, raisins, pennies, buttons, and marbles. There should be 40–70 objects each time your child groups and counts.

Thank you for your cooperation.

Ask an adult or an older sister or brother to help you find objects to count.

Object	Number of Groups of 10	Number of Leftovers	Number

Return this paper on _____ .

How Many Letters?

Homework

Write the number of letters in the first names of four people or pets at home.

First Name	Number of Letters

Total Number of Letters = _____

Draw a picture or tell how you found the total number of letters.

Return this sheet to school by _____ .

Spin for Beans 50

Materials

Spin for Beans 50 Playing Mat

Spin for Beans 50 Recording Sheet

50 baby lima beans for each player

clear plastic spinner or a pencil and paper clip

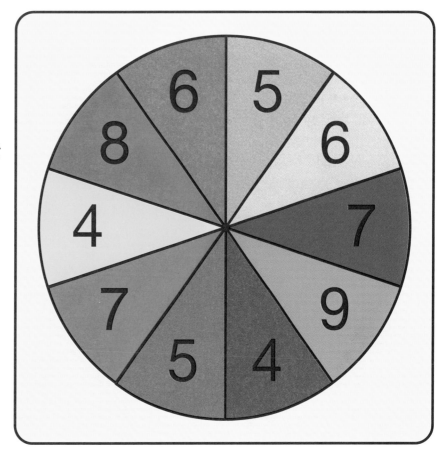

Directions

1. Place a plastic spinner over the spinner above. If you do not have a clear spinner, use a pencil and a paper clip.

2. Spin to find out how many beans to take.

3. Place the beans on the ten frame, one in each square on the playing mat.

4. Write the number of tens you have on your recording sheet. Write the number of leftover ones you have, too.

5. Write the total number of beans you have.

6. Each time you spin, add the beans to your collection on the ten frames until someone collects 50 beans.

Spin for Beans at Home

Homework

Dear Family Member:

Your child has played the game *Spin for Beans 50* in school and is ready to teach it to someone at home. You may use coins, paper clips, several scraps of paper, or other small counters instead of beans. Please help your child keep a record of the number of minutes he or she plays and the number of people she or he teaches to play the game.

Thank you for your cooperation.

Make a tally mark for each person you teach to play the game.

Tallies _____

Make a tally mark for every five minutes you play the game.

Tallies _____   Total Minutes _____

Parent's Signature _____

Child's Signature _____

Return this sheet to school by _____ .

50 Chart

<table>
<tr><td></td><td></td><td></td><td></td><td></td></tr>
<tr><td></td><td></td><td></td><td></td><td></td></tr>
<tr><td></td><td></td><td></td><td></td><td></td></tr>
<tr><td></td><td></td><td></td><td></td><td></td></tr>
<tr><td></td><td></td><td></td><td></td><td></td></tr>
<tr><td></td><td></td><td></td><td></td><td></td></tr>
<tr><td></td><td></td><td></td><td></td><td></td></tr>
<tr><td></td><td></td><td></td><td></td><td></td></tr>
<tr><td></td><td></td><td></td><td></td><td></td></tr>
<tr><td></td><td></td><td></td><td></td><td></td></tr>
</table>

100 Chart

1	2	3	4	5	6	7	8	9	10
11	12	13	14	15	16	17	18	19	20
21	22	23	24	25	26	27	28	29	30
31	32	33	34	35	36	37	38	39	40
41	42	43	44	45	46	47	48	49	50
51	52	53	54	55	56	57	58	59	60
61	62	63	64	65	66	67	68	69	70
71	72	73	74	75	76	77	78	79	80
81	82	83	84	85	86	87	88	89	90
91	92	93	94	95	96	97	98	99	100

Counting by Tens

Homework

Count by tens and fill in the missing numbers. Use the *100 Chart* to help you. Color each column on the *100 Chart* using the colors below.

yellow	green	orange	blue	red	purple
8	10	2			
18					
28			25		
38					36
				51	

Guess My Number

Homework

Dear Family Member:

Your child is learning about locating and placing numbers in intervals. Help your child locate numbers in intervals by playing "Guess My Number." Your child has practiced this game in class. The rules are listed below. We recommend that you use numbers that are between 1 and 20 to start.

Thank you for your cooperation.

For two or more players.

Rules:

- Player 1: Selects a number.

  For example, "I am thinking of a number that is between _____ and _____ ."

- Player 2: Tries to guess the number Player 1 has selected.

- Player 1: Corrects Player 2's guess by saying either "It is lower" or "It is higher."

- Player 2: Continues to make guesses as Player 1 continues to give out clues.

Play ends when Player 2 guesses the number.

Players can use a calendar, a *100 Chart,* or a centimeter ruler to help find the number.

Find Numbers in the News

Homework

Dear Family Member:

Help your child find a newspaper headline with a number on it. Glue the headline in the space provided on the back of this paper. If your child cannot find one in the newspaper, circle one of the headlines below.

To get your child started, write one sentence that compares the number to other numbers. For example, 34 is 10 more than 24. More examples are listed for the number 34 below.

Encourage your child to think of his or her own sentences. He or she should record them on the lines provided on the back of this paper.

Thank you for your cooperation.

13-Hour Sale

32 TOTAL BODY EXERCISES

Dist. 87 gets tougher on bad checks

75 years later, medals honor veterans of World War I

34 Kids Think in Math Marathon

34 is
- large compared to 5;
- about the same size as 30;
- a lot less than 100;
- between 30 and 40;
- 10 more than 24;
- 10 less than 44;
- 1 more than 33;
- 1 less than 35.

Paste your headline below.

_____

_____

_____

_____

_____

_____

_____

_____

_____

Numbers in the News

Full of Beans

Draw a picture of the lab setup.

Collect

Write the kind of bean and the number of beans you counted in this table.

Group Data Table

Kind of Bean	Number of Beans

Class Data Table

Kind of Bean	Number of Beans

Full of Beans Class Data

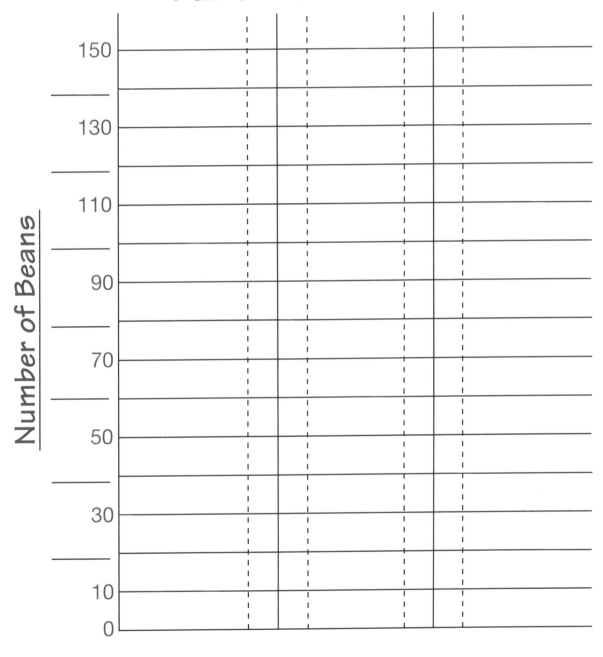

1. Which kind of bean did your cup hold more of?

    _____

    About how many more of that kind of bean did the cup hold
    than the other kind? Use your graph to help you.

    _____

2. Which kind of bean was bigger?

    _____

3. Will a cup always hold more small beans than big beans?
    Explain your answer.

    _____

    _____

    _____

4. Work with your partner to answer this question. Then, tell the
    rest of the class how you found your answer.

    If we had a big cup that holds 200 of the small beans, about
    how many large beans would the cup hold?

    _____

Maria and José's Graph

Maria and José did the *Full of Beans* experiment with lima beans and kidney beans. Here is a bar graph of their data.

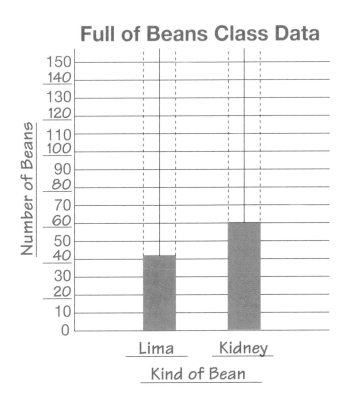

Full of Beans Class Data

1. About how many lima beans were in the cup? _____

2. Which beans were bigger, the lima or the kidney beans?

   _____

3. About how many more kidney beans were there than lima beans?

   _____

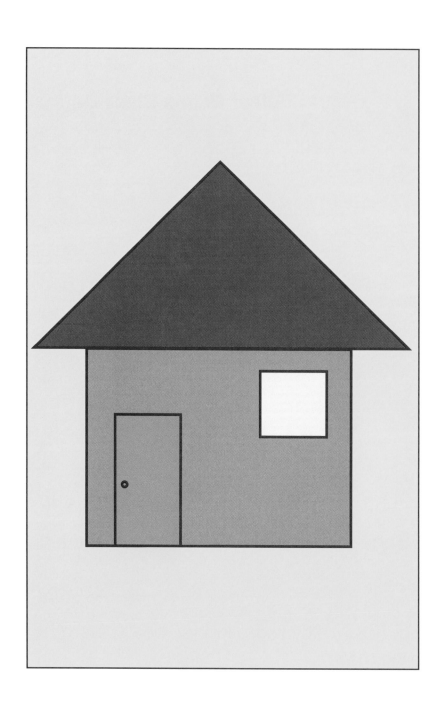

Unit 10
MEASUREMENT: AREA

	Student Guide	Adventure Book	Unit Resource Guide*
Lesson 1			
Finding Area with Pennies	◎		
Lesson 2			
Goldilocks and the Three Rectangles	◎		
Lesson 3			
How Much Area?	◎		
Lesson 4			
The Midnight Visit		◎	
Lesson 5			
Unit Designs	◎		

Unit Resource Guide pages are from the teacher materials.

Partly Cloudy

More Clouds

Cloud A

How many pennies? _____

Cloud B

How many pennies? _____

Draw a Shape

Homework

Dear Family Member:

In class your child measured the area of shapes by counting the number of pennies needed to cover each shape. Please gather pennies and quarters for your child so he or she may have more practice finding area. Help your child complete the questions below. Thank you.

Draw a large shape in the space below. Then, answer the questions.

1. Cover the shape with pennies. How many cover the shape?

_____

2. Cover the shape with quarters. How many cover the shape?

_____

3. Did more pennies or more quarters fit in the shape? Explain why you think more of this coin fit in the shape.

_____

Goldilocks and the Three Rectangles

The Three Rectangles

Randy Rectangle

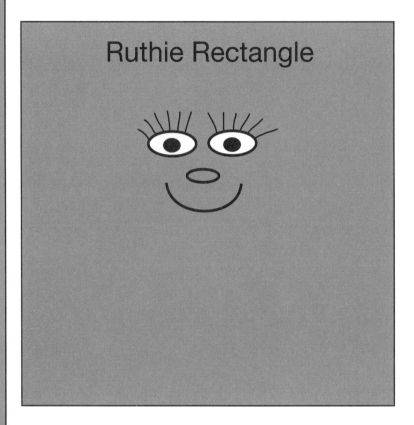

Ruthie Rectangle

Rebecca Rectangle

Rectangle Table

Record Randy's, Rebecca's, and Ruthie's measurements in the table below.

Name	Tall (in inches)	Wide (in inches)	Area (in square inches)
Randy			
Rebecca			
Ruthie			

Rupert Rectangle

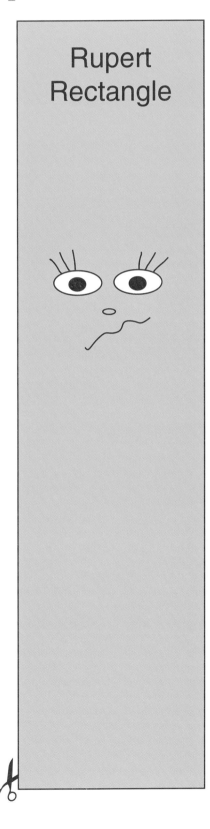

Rupert
Rectangle

Square Inches

Tiles 1

Find and record the area of each figure below. Use square-inch tiles and halves of square-inch tiles to help you.

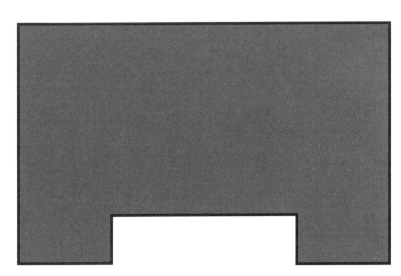

1. _____ square inches

2. _____ square inches

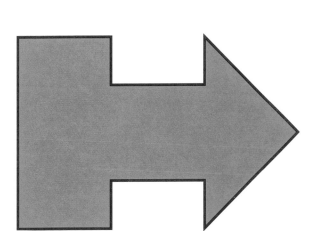

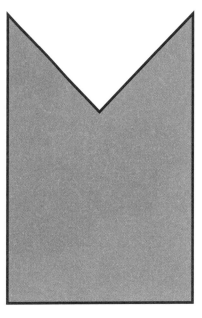

3. _____ square inches

4. _____ square inches

Tiles 2

Find and record the area of each figure below. Use square-inch tiles and halves of square-inch tiles to help you.

1. _____ square inches

2. _____ square inches

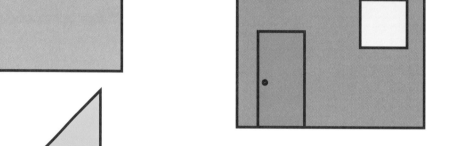

3. _____ square inches

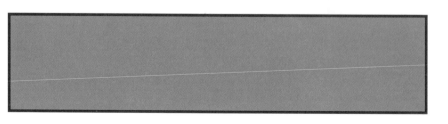

4. _____ square inches

Tiles 3

What is the area of each shape?
Use square-inch tiles and halves
of square-inch tiles to help you.

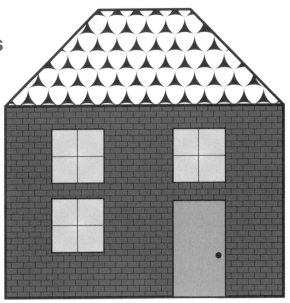

1. _____ square inches

2. _____ square inches

3. _____ square inches

Unit Designs

Homework

Dear Family Member:

In class your child created a design similar to those below using square-inch and half-square-inch pieces. To find the area of the shapes, your child will count full square inches and piece half-square inches together to make more wholes. Check that your child records the area for each shape and includes the unit of measure, "square inches." Thank you.

Find the area of each of the shapes below. Include in your answer the number and unit.

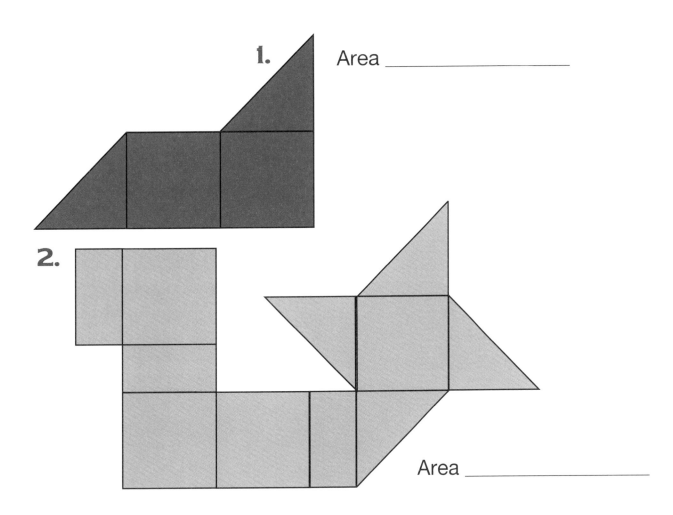

1. Area _____

2. Area _____

3.

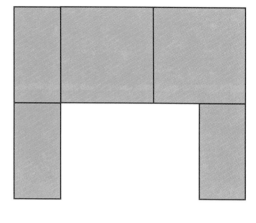

Area _____

4.

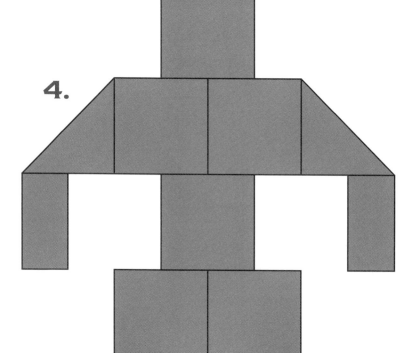

Area _____

Which Two?

Find which two shapes have the same area. There is one shape on the next page.

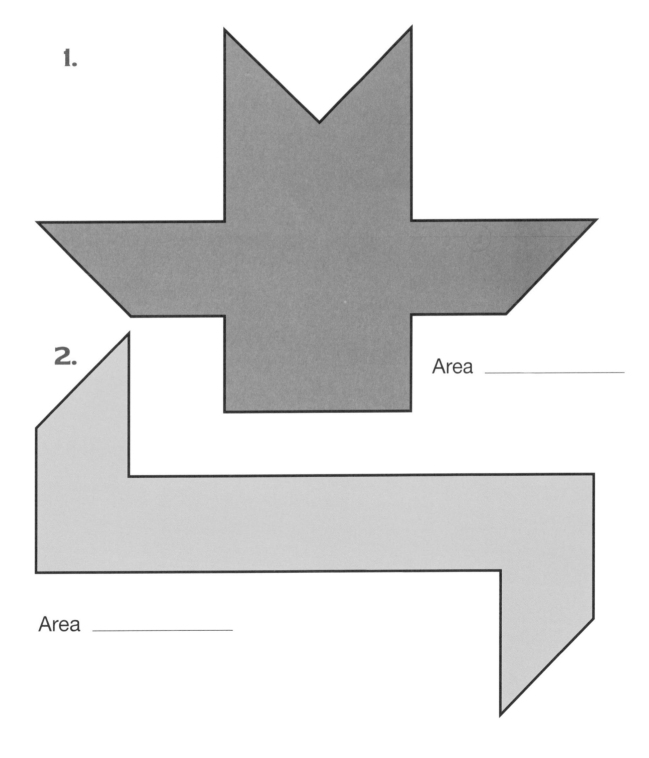

1.

Area _____

2.

Area _____

3.

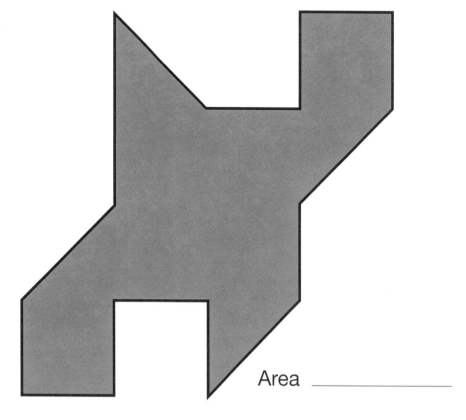

Area _____

4. Which two shapes have the same area?

_____

5. Does the other shape have a larger or smaller area than the two shapes with the same area?

_____

Glossary

This glossary provides definitions of key terms in the Grade 1 lessons as a resource for teachers and parents.

A

Area (Unit 10)
The amount of space that a shape covers. Area is measured in square units.

B

C

Circumference (Unit 15)
The distance around a circle.

Counting All (Unit 1)
A strategy for counting and adding in which students start at one and count until the total is reached.

Counting On (Unit 1, Unit 4)
A strategy for counting or adding objects in which students start from a larger number and then count until the total is reached. For example, to count $6 + 3$, begin with 6 and count three more, 7, 8, 9.

Cube (Unit 12, Unit 15)
A solid with six congruent square faces.

Cubic Units (Unit 12)
A unit for measuring volume—a cube that measures one unit along each edge. For example, cubic centimeters and cubic inches are standard units of measure.

cubic centimeter

Cylinder (Unit 15)
A three-dimensional figure with two parallel congruent circles as bases (top and bottom) and a curved side which is the union of parallel lines connecting corresponding points on the circles.

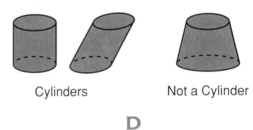

Cylinders   Not a Cylinder

D

Data Table
A tool for recording and organizing information.

Name	Age

E

Edge (Unit 15)
A line segment where two faces of a three-dimensional figure meet.

Estimate (Unit 12)
1. To find *about* how many (as a verb).
2. An approximate number (as a noun).

Even Number (Unit 4)
Numbers that are doubles. The numbers 0, 2, 4, 6, 8, 10, . . . etc. are even. The number 28 is even because it is 14 + 14.

F

Face (Unit 12)
A flat side of a three-dimensional figure.

Fixed Variables (Unit 2, Unit 11)
Variables in an experiment that do not change.

G

H

Hexagon (Unit 2)
A six-sided polygon.

Hexagons   Not Hexagons

I

J

K

L

Length
The distance along a line or curve from one point to another. Distance can be measured with a ruler or tape measure. Distance can also be measured in paces, handspans, and other non-standard units.

Line
A set of points that form a straight path extending infinitely in two directions.

Line Symmetry (Unit 7, Unit 18)
A figure has line symmetry if it can be folded along a line so that the two halves match exactly.

Line of Symmetry (Unit 7)
A line such that if a figure is folded along the line, then one half of the figure matches the other.

M

Making a Ten (Unit 13)
A strategy for adding and subtracting that takes advantage of students' knowledge of partitions of ten. For example, a student might find 8 + 4 by breaking the 4 into 2 + 2 and then using a knowledge of sums that add to ten.

$$8 + 4 =$$
$$8 + 2 + 2 =$$
$$10 + 2 = 12$$

Median (Unit 6, Unit 9)
The number "in the middle" of a set of data. If there are an odd number of data, it is the number in the middle when the numbers are arranged in order. So the median of $\{1, 2, 14, 15, 28, 29, 30\}$ is 15. If there are an even number of data, it is the number halfway between the two middle numbers. The median of $\{1, 2, 14, 15, 28, 29\}$ is $14\frac{1}{2}$.

Mr. Origin (Unit 6, Unit 9)
A plastic figure used to help children learn about direction and distance.

N

Near Double (Unit 13)
A derived addition or subtraction fact found by using doubles. For example, $3 + 4 = 7$ follows from the fact that $3 + 3 = 6$.

Number Sentence (Unit 3)
A number sentence uses numbers and symbols instead of words to describe a problem. For example, a number sentence for the problem "Five birds landed on a branch. Two more birds also landed on the branch. How many birds are on the branch?" is $5 + 2 = 7$.

O

Odd Number (Unit 4)
A number that is not even. The odd numbers are 1, 3, 5, 7, 9, and so on.

Origin (Unit 6, Unit 9)
A reference point for a coordinate system. If the coordinate system is a line, we can determine the location of an object on the line by the number of units it is to the right or the left of the origin.

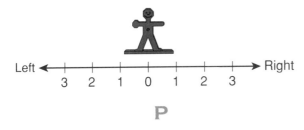

P

Pattern Unit (Unit 7)
The portion of a pattern that is repeated. For example, AAB is the pattern unit in the pattern AABAABAAB.

Perimeter (Unit 6)
The distance around a two-dimensional shape.

Polygon
A closed, connected plane figure consisting of line segments, with exactly two segments meeting at each end point.

Polygons   Not Polygons

Prediction (Unit 5)
Using a sample to tell about what is likely to occur in a population.

Prism (Unit 15)
A solid that has two congruent and parallel bases. The remaining faces (sides) are parallelograms. For example, a rectangular prism has bases that are rectangles. A box is a common object that is shaped like a rectangular prism.

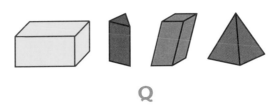

Q

Quadrilateral
A polygon with four sides.

Quadrilaterals   Not a Quadrilateral

R

Rectangle (Unit 2)
A quadrilateral with four right angles.

Rectangles   Not a Rectangle

Rhombus (Unit 2)
A quadrilateral with four sides of equal length.

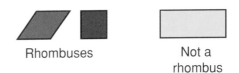

Rhombuses   Not a rhombus

S

Sample (Unit 5)
Some of the items from a collection.

Sphere (Unit 15)
A three-dimensional figure that is made up of points that are the same distance from one point, the center. A basketball is a common object shaped like a sphere.

Square (Unit 2)
A rectangle with four equal sides.

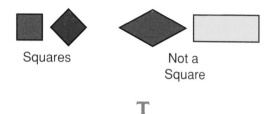

Squares   Not a
                 Square

T

Three-dimensional Shapes (Unit 15)
A geometric solid. A figure in space that has length, width, and height.

TIMS Laboratory Method
A method that students use to organize experiments and investigations. It involves four components: draw, collect, graph, and explore. It is a way to help students learn about the scientific method. TIMS is an acronym for Teaching Integrated Mathematics and Science.

Trapezoid (Unit 2)
A quadrilateral with exactly one pair of parallel sides.

Trial (Unit 6)
One attempt in an experiment.

Triangle (Unit 2)
A polygon with three sides.

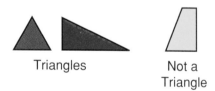

Triangles   Not a
                   Triangle

U

Using Doubles (Unit 13)
A strategy for adding and subtracting that uses facts derived from known doubles. For example, students use $7 + 7 = 14$ to find that $7 + 8$ is one more, or 15.

Using Ten (Unit 13)
A strategy for adding and subtracting which uses reasoning from known facts. For example, students use $3 + 7 = 10$ to find that $4 + 7$ is one more, or 11.

V

Variable (Unit 2, Unit 11)
A variable is something that can vary or change in an experiment.

Volume (Unit 9, Unit 12)
1. The amount of space an object takes up.
2. The amount of space inside a container (also called capacity).

W

X

Y

Z

GRADE

Index

The index provides page references for the *Student Guide.* Definition or explanation of key terms can be found in the glossary. A good source for information on the location of topics in the curriculum is the *Scope and Sequence* in Section 5 of the *Teacher Implementation Guide.*

100 Chart, 167, 217
    Arrow Dynamics Game and, 215–223
50 Chart, empty, 165

Addition, 32–65, 72, 81, 263–289. *See also* Counting, Games, Number Sentences, Word Problems
    counting on strategy, 77–79
    doubling numbers as, 265–277, 287
    graphs and, 283–284
    and money, 81
    number sentences, 49–51, 205–210, 212–213
    problem solving with, 72–74, 279–281, 285, 289, 308–311, 405, 411
    stories, 73–74, 267–268
    tens and hundreds, 355–356
Area, 182–202
    comparing, 187–191, 201–202
    counting square units and half-square units, 187–202, 246, 410
    of irregular shapes, 182–185
    with nonstandard units, 182–185
    problem solving with, 410
    of rectangles, 187–191
    square inch tiles for, 193–200
Arrow Dynamics Game, 215–223

Balancing Act Game, 145
Bar graphs, 105–106, 109, 239. *See also* Labs
    making, 28, 106, 177, 231
    reading, 179, 283–284, 297
    telling a story, 341, 345

Calculator, keystrokes, 72
Calendar, 77, 408
    and counting on strategy, 77
    weather, 25–29, 227
Circles, 359, 362, 363
    in fraction puzzles, 375–377
Circumference, of cylinder, 317–318
Colors Lab, 93–97
Comparing
    area, 187–191, 201–202
    length, 7–9, 119–121, 317–318
    more than/less than, 7, 9, 187–191, 247, 249, 255, 261
    numbers, 7–9, 187–191, 247, 249, 255, 261
    shapes, 15–17, 313
    volumes, 247, 249, 255, 261
    weather, 239–241
Counting, 3–5, 9, 37
    by fives and tens, 87, 353–354
    and grouping, 83–97, 160–161
    hundreds, 348–354
    and multiplication, 295–299
    with tallies, 27, 32–33, 164
    by tens, 167–169, 348–351
    by twos, 84–85, 351
Counting all strategy, 2–3, 5
Counting on strategy, 77–79
    on the calendar, 77
Counting up strategy, 157
Cubes, 313, 319–324
    identifying, 321–323
Cubic units, 246, 249
Cylinders (tubes), 313, 315–319, 321, 323–324

Data Table, 3, 5, 27, 32–33, 57, 59–63, 111, 117, 141, 161, 189, 230, 233, 253, 316, 318, 326, 337, 400–401. *See also* Labs
Digit cards, 264
Dimes, 206–207, 209–210, 401
Directions, left, right, 392–401
   left, right, front, back, 393
Distance, measuring, 103–111, 117
Division, 299, 301–302, 305, 407, 409, 412, 414
   and money, 301
   by sharing, 89–91, 301, 305
   stories, 89, 299, 407, 412
Doubling, 265–277, 287
Doubles Railroad Game, 269–275
Drawing a picture, *See* Labs

Even and odd numbers, 68–69, 279–281

Fifty, partitioning, 213
Fifty chart, 165
Foods
   favorite, 331
   groups, 333–338
   healthy, 339–341
   serving sizes of, 338
Fourths, 363–369, 373, 383–385
Fractional part of a collection, 387–388
Fractions, 359–389
   equal shares, 369–373, 389
   fourths, 363–369, 373, 383–385
   fraction puzzles, 375–385
   halves, 193–202, 269–277, 359–362, 367–371, 383
Full of Beans Lab, 175–179

Games
   Arrow Dynamics, 215–223
   Balancing Act, 145
   Doubles Railroad, 269–275
   Guess My Number, 171
   How Many in the Bag, 157
   Make Ten, 264
   Mr. Origin Says, 393
   Spin for Beans 50 Game, 163–165
   Think and Spin Game, 41
Graph, *See* Bar Graph
Geometry, *See* Shapes, Line symmetry, Length, Area, Volume
Grouping, 89–91, 159–179, 405
   counting and, 83–97, 160–161
   counting by tens and, 167–169
   Full of Beans Lab, 175–179
   Guess My Number Game, 171
   number comparisons, 173–174
   Spin for Beans 50 Game, 163–165
   by tens, 160, 163–165, 348–351
Guess My Number Game, 171

Halves, 193–202, 269–277, 359–362, 367–371, 383
   of numbers, 269–275, 277
   shapes, 359–362, 367–371, 383–385
Healthy Kids Lab, 337–345
Height, 246, 255–257, 317–318
Hexagons, 15, 19–23
   with fractions, 361, 365
How Many in the Bag Game, 157
Hundreds, 348–356
   addition of, 355–356
   counting, 348–354

Inches, 123, 188–189
Intervals, 171

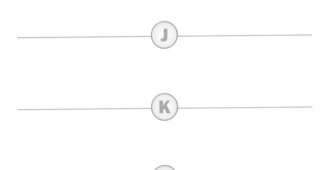

J

K

L

Labs (TIMS Laboratory Investigations)
   Colors, 93–97
   Full of Beans, 175–179
   Healthy Kids, 337–345
   Mr. Origin Left/Right, 395–401
   Pets, 295–299
   Pocket Parts, 47–53
   Rolling Along with Links, 103–109
   Weather 1: Eye on the Sky, 25–29
   Weather 2: Winter Skies, 227–239
   What's in That Pocket, 55–63
Left/right direction, 392–401
Leftover numbers, 69, 89–91, 160
Length, 100–123, 317–318, 392–401, 404.
      See also Mapping
   comparing, 7–9, 119–121, 317–318
   distance as, 103–111, 117
   estimating, 123
   in inches, 123, 188–189
   with links, 7, 9, 100–109, 392–401
   with nonstandard units, 7–9, 100–109, 111–121,
      392–401
Line symmetry, 139–140, 143–145, 359–366

M

Make Ten Game, 264
Making a ten, 167–169, 348–351
Mapping, One-dimension, 392–401
Measurement, *See also* Length, Area, and Volume
   comparing units, 117–121
Money, 79–81, 141, 205–213, 401
   addition and, 81
   division and, 301
   Problem solving with coins, 65, 141, 205–211

Mr. Origin, 392–401
Mr. Origin Left/Right Lab, 395–401
Mr. Origin Says Game, 393
Multiplication and division word problems, 293–294,
    299–305, 409, 412, 414

N

Name grid pattern, 133–137
Nickels, 211, 213, 401
Number line, 395–401
Number relationships, 167–173, 204–213
Number sentences
   addition, 49–51, 205–210, 212–213
   for doubles, 267–268
   for ten frames, 38–39
   for tens, 205–206
   solving, 408, 410, 413, 415
   subtraction, 149–158, 205–206, 209–210
   writing, 38–39, 47–65, 75, 77, 173, 205–215,
     219–220, 243
Numbers, *See also* Partitioning
   comparisons of, 7–9, 187–191, 247, 249, 255, 261
   doubling, 265, 267–277, 287
   even and odd, 68–69, 279–281
   halving, 269–277
   leftover, 69, 89–91, 160

O

Odd and even numbers, 68–69, 279–281
One hundred
   Arrow Dynamics Game and, 215–223
   chart, 167, 217
   partitioning, 204–212
   time units of, 225
Ovals, 375–377

P

Partitioning
    numbers, 47–63, 75, 148, 404
    fifty, 213
    one hundred, 204–212
Part-part-whole problems, 49–63, 75, 148–153, 404
Patterns
    in colors and shapes, 127–131
    name grid, 133–137
    pattern blocks and, 20–23, 145
    problem solving with, 406, 411
    repeating, 126–131, 406
    translating/recording, 126
Perimeter, 100
Pictures, *See* Labs
Pets Lab, 295–299
Pocket Parts Lab, 47–53
Prediction, 97, 119–121. *See also* Labs
Prisms (boxes), 313, 319, 321, 323–324
Problem posing, 65, 296, 330
Problem solving, 65, 72–74, 237–238, 279–289,
        308–311, 328–330, 403–415. *See also* Labs,
        Word Problems
    with addition, 72–74, 279–281, 285, 289, 308–311
    with area, 410
    with coins, 65, 141, 205–211
    with multiplication, 303–305
    with subtraction, 151–153, 279–281, 285, 289,
        308–311, 328–330, 405
    with volume, 412–413
    using weather, 237–238

Q

Quarters (coins), 212–213

R

Rectangles, 13–15, 187–191, 359–366, 379–381
  in fraction puzzles, 379–381
Rhombus, 20–23
Rolling along with Links Lab, 103–109

S

Samples, 94–97
Shapes, *See also* Line symmetry
    comparing/contrasting, 15–17, 313
    covering/construction, 19–23
    cubes, 313, 319–324
        identifying, 321–323
    cylinders (tubes), 313, 315–319, 321, 323–324
    halves of, 359–362, 367–371, 383–385
    hexagons, 15, 19–23
    identifying, 12–13, 321–325
    with pattern blocks, 19–23
    patterns with, 127–131
    prisms (boxes), 313, 319, 321, 323–324
    properties, 15–17, 313, 317–318
    rectangles, 13–15, 187–191, 359–366, 379–381
    squares, 13, 20–23
    three-dimensional, 246–261, 313–326, *See also*
        cubes, cylinders (tubes), prisms (boxes),
        spheres (balls)
    trapezoids, 20–23
    triangles, 13, 17, 19–23
    two-dimensional, 12–23
Skip counting
    by tens, 87, 90–91, 167–169, 349–351
    by twos, 84–85
Sorting, 333–334
Spheres (balls), 313, 321–325
Spin for Beans 50 Game, 163–165
Square inch tiles, 193–202
Squares, 13, 20–23
  and fractions, 359–365, 371–373, 379–381
Subtraction, 148–153, 404. *See also* Word Problems,
        Part-Part-Whole Problems
    counting up/back, 157
    halving numbers as, 277
    number sentences, 149–158, 205–206, 209–210
    problem solving with, 151–153, 279–281, 285, 289,
        308–311, 328–330, 405
Survey, 331, 337
Symmetry, *See* Line symmetry

Tallying, 27, 32–33, 164, 242–243, 337, 343
Ten Frames, 35–43, 87
   empty, 35, 43
   in identifying numbers, 37
Tens
   counting by, 87, 90–91, 167–169, 264, 279–281,
      348–351
   grouping by, 160, 163–165, 348–351
Think and Spin Game, 41
TIMS Laboratory Investigations, *See* Labs
Trapezoid, 20–23
Triangles, 13, 17, 19–23
   and fractions, 359, 362, 371

U.S. Department of Agriculture, 338
Units, *See* Length, Area, and Volume
USA map, 241

Weather, 25–29, 227–239
   calendar for recording, 25–29, 227
   comparing, 239–241
   problem solving using, 237–238
Weather 1: Eye on the Sky Lab, 25–29
Weather 2: Winter Skies Lab, 229–239
What's in That Pocket Lab, 55–63
Whole-Part-Part mat, 148
Word problems, 279–281, 285, 289, 293–294,
      299–305, 328–329, 405, 406, 409, 412,
      413, 414. *See also* Labs

Volume, 246–261
   comparing, 247, 249, 255, 261
   cube models and, 246–249
   of cubic animals, 259–261
   estimating, 247–249
   problem solving with, 412–413